Ghost Shortbread Cookies

Halloween Black Cat Cookies

Day of the Dead Cookies

Pumpkin Cookie Pops

Bloody Bones Cookies

Gingerbread Skeletons

Chocolate Peanut Butter Owl Cookies

Oreo Pumpkin Cookie Balls

Chocolate Bat Cookies

Introduction

Halloween is one the most festive and enjoyable times of year. There are many parties, trick-or-treats, candy, and cookies. Halloween is magical with goblins, ghosts, witches, and pumpkins. You will love Halloween parties if you are a fan. These parties should have their own cookies.

This book contains many Halloween-themed cookies in fun shapes, with Halloween-themed ingredients like candy corn and pumpkin.

Enjoy!

Pumpkin Chocolate Chip Cookies

Ingredients:

1/2 cup shortening
1 1/2 cups white sugar
1 egg
1 cup canned pumpkin
1 tsp. vanilla extract
2 1/2 cups all-purpose flour
1 tsp. baking powder
1 tsp. baking soda
1 tsp. salt
1 tsp. ground nutmeg
1 tsp. ground cinnamon
1/2 cup chopped walnuts (optional)
1 cup semisweet chocolate chips

Directions:

1. Preheat oven to 350°F (175° C).
2. Grease cookie sheets
3. Combine the sugar and shortening in a large bowl until it is light and fluffy. Mix in the egg and then add the pumpkin and vanilla.
4. Mix the flour, baking powder and baking soda together with the cinnamon. Add the mixture to the creamed mixture.
5. Add the chocolate chips and walnuts to the mixture.
6. Drop the dough in teaspoonfuls onto prepared cookie sheets.
7. Bake for 15 minutes or until the top is light brown.
8. Cool wire racks

Pumpkin Oatmeal Chocolate Chip Cookies

Ingredients:

1 1/2 cups butter, softened
2 cups packed brown sugar
1 cup white sugar
1 (15 oz.) can pumpkin puree
1 egg
1 tsp. vanilla extract
4 cups all-purpose flour
2 cups quick-cooking oats
2 tsps. ground cinnamon
2 tsps. baking soda
1 tsp. baking powder
1 tsp. salt
2 cups miniature chocolate chips

Directions:

1. Preheat oven to 375°F (190° C).
2. Combine butter, brown sugar, white sugar and salt in a bowl. Beat until smooth. Blend in the pumpkin, egg and vanilla extract.
3. Combine flour, oats and cinnamon in a separate bowl. Stir into creamed butter until well combined.
4. Incorporate chocolate chips in the batter. Drop 1 to 2 tablespoons. Place the batter for each cookie on a baking sheet.
5. Bake the cookies in the oven for 10-12 minutes, or until they are lightly browned around the edges.

Edible Spiders

Ingredients:

1 cup semisweet chocolate chips
1 tsp. butter
24 large marshmallows
1 (6 oz.) package chow mein noodles
1 (12 oz.) package mini candy-coated chocolate pieces

Directions:

1. Combine butter and chocolate chips in a microwave-safe bowl. Microwave until melted. Stir frequently until the chocolate is smooth.
2. Place the chocolate in a plastic bag.
3. Place wax paper on a cookie sheet.
4. For legs, stick 4 chow mein noodles on each marshmallow side and place them on wax paper.
5. Cut one corner of the bag with scissors.
6. Sprinkle the marshmallow spiders with honey.
7. For eyes, attach 2 marshmallows with candy candies.
8. Allow chocolate to harden in the refrigerator.

Halloween Nutt Butter Ghosts

Ingredients:

1 (12 oz.) pkg. white chocolate chips, or as needed
24 peanut-shaped peanut butter sandwich cookies
48 miniature chocolate chips

Directions:

1. Mix the chocolate chips in a microwave-safe bowl. Heat on low for 1 minute. Stir.
2. Keep heating the white chocolate on low for 30 seconds more, stirring every time.
3. To dip white chocolate cookies in, use 2 forks
4. Place cookies on waxed papers.
5. For eyes, place 2 mini chocolate chips on each cookie's end. Leave cookies alone for 20 minutes until the coating is set.

Acorn Candy Cookies

Ingredients:

1 tbsp. prepared chocolate frosting
24 milk chocolate candy kisses (such as Hershey's Kisses®), unwrapped
24 mini vanilla wafer cookies (such as Nilla®)
24 butterscotch chips

Directions:

1. Spread a little frosting on the bottom of a candy-shaped kiss.
2. Place the vanilla wafer flat on the bottom.
3. Spread a little frosting on the flat bottom of the butterscotch chips and then press the cookie's rounded top.
4. Continue with the remaining ingredients. Allow to dry for about 30 minutes

Witches' Hats

Ingredients:

2 (16 oz.) pkg. fudge stripe cookies
1/4 cup honey, or as needed
1 (9 oz.) bag milk chocolate candy kisses, unwrapped
1 (4.5 oz.) tube decorating gel

Directions:

1. Place a fudge stripe cookie, bottom side up, on a work surface.
2. Use a tiny dab (1/8 teaspoon) of honey to coat your lips. Place a small amount of honey on the bottom of a chocolate cookie. Secure the candy piece in the middle of the cookie by securing it, closing the hole.
3. You can pipe a small bow on the bottom of the candy pieces using decorating gel.
4. Continue with the remaining ingredients.

Owl Cookies

Ingredients:

1 cup white sugar
3/4 cup butter
1 egg
1 tsp. vanilla extract
2 1/4 cups all-purpose flour
2 tsps. baking powder
1/2 tsp. salt
3 tbsps. unsweetened cocoa powder
1 cup semisweet chocolate chips
1 cup cashew halves

Directions:

1. Blend butter and sugar together until smooth.
2. Mix in the egg and vanilla.
3. Add baking powder and salt.
4. Beat well.
5. Mix flour with water until well combined
6. Take out 2/3 of the dough.
7. To form two rectangles of 10x4 inches, roll or pat the dough.
8. To the remaining 1/3 of the dough, add cocoa.
9. Mix until blended.
10. Make two 10-inch long rolls from the chocolate dough.
11. Place the rectangle on a flat surface and roll out plain dough.
12. Wrap in plastic wrap, and chill for at least two hours
13. Preheat oven to 350°F (180° C).
14. Use a sharp knife to cut the dough into 1-inch slices.
15. To resemble an owl's head, place two slices side-by-side on a cookie sheet. To resemble ears, pinch the upper "corners".
16. For eyes, place chocolate chips in each circle. Then add a cashew in its center to make the beak.
17. Bake for 8-12 minutes in the preheated baking oven or until lightly browned.

Peanut Butter Spider Cookies

Ingredients:

1/2 cup shortening
1/2 cup peanut butter
1/2 cup packed brown sugar
1/2 cup white sugar
1 egg, beaten
2 tbsps. milk
1 tsp. vanilla extract
1 3/4 cups all-purpose flour
1 tsp. baking soda
1/2 tsp. salt
1/4 cup white sugar for rolling
24 chocolate candy truffles with chocolate filling, refrigerated until cold
48 decorative candy eyeballs
1/2 cup prepared chocolate frosting

Directions:

1. Preheat oven to 375°F (190° C).
2. Bake parchment on baking sheets.
3. Blend shortening, peanut butter and 1/2 cup brown sugar with an electric mixer until smooth.
4. Mix the egg in with the cream mixture until it is fully combined.
5. Mix milk and vanilla extract until the mixture is smooth.
6. Combine flour, baking soda and salt in a small bowl. Add to the large bowl with the wet mixture and stir until it becomes a dough.
7. Divide the dough into 48 balls and form it.
8. In a large, shallow bowl, add 1/4 cup of white sugar.
9. To coat the dough balls, roll them in sugar and place 2 inches apart on prepared baking sheets.
10. Bake in the oven for 10-12 minutes or until golden brown.
11. Take out the cookies from the oven. Use a blunt end of a spoon to quickly make a dent in the middle of each cookie.
12. Allow cookies to cool on sheets for 10 minutes, then transfer to a wire cooling rack.
13. Each chocolate sphere should be cut into two hemispheres.
14. Place one piece on top of each cookie, with the round side facing upwards.
15. Use a pastry bag or plastic freezer bag to spoon the frosting.
16. To make eyes, drizzle a little frosting on the back of each candy eyeball. Stick two of them onto each chocolate candy.
17. Pipe frosting along four lines starting at the bottom of the candy and ending at each end. This will give the cookie the appearance of spider legs.
18. Frosting should set at room temperature for approximately 30 minutes.

Meringue Bones

Ingredients:

6 egg whites
1/2 tsp. cream of tartar
1 pinch salt
1 1/3 cups white sugar
2 tsps. vanilla extract

Directions:
1. Preheat oven to 225°F (110°C).
2. Line two baking sheets with aluminum foil, and then grease the foil.
3. Mix egg whites, cream of tartar, salt and a bowl using an electric mixer. Beat eggs until foamy
4. Gradually add sugar, a few tablespoons. Beat one at a time until sugar dissolves in meringue.
5. Continue beating the meringue until it is glossy. When beaters lift the bowl out of the bowl, the peak will form. Add vanilla extract.
6. Place the meringue in a bag with a tip.
7. Pipe meringue in small shapes onto the aluminum foil. Pipe all shapes simultaneously or your meringue may deflate.
8. Bake for one hour in a preheated oven by placing cookie sheets on baking sheets.
9. Do not open oven door or peek during baking.
10. Turn off the oven and allow the meringue to cool in the oven for at least 1 hour.
11. To prevent broken bones, gently and gently remove aluminum cookies.

Iced Pumpkin Cookies

Ingredients:

2 1/2 cups all-purpose flour
1 tsp. baking powder
1 tsp. baking soda
2 tsps. ground cinnamon
1/2 tsp. ground nutmeg
1/2 tsp. ground cloves
1/2 tsp. salt
1/2 cup butter, softened
1 1/2 cups white sugar
1 cup canned pumpkin puree
1 egg
1 tsp. vanilla extract
2 cups confectioners' sugar
3 tbsps. milk
1 tbsp. melted butter
1 tsp. vanilla extract

Directions:

1. Preheat oven to 350°F (175° C).
2. Mix flour, baking powder and baking soda with cinnamon, nutmeg and ground cloves. Set aside.
3. Mix 1/2 cup butter and the white sugar in a large bowl. Mix in the pumpkin, egg, and 1 teaspoon of salt. Add vanilla to butter mixture and beat until smooth. Mix in dry ingredients.
4. Drop tablespoonfuls of cookies onto a cookie sheet; flatten slightly.
5. Bake for 15 to 20 mins in the preheated oven
6. Let cool cookies cool, then drizzle glaze using a fork.
7. To make Glaze: Mix confectioners' sugar and milk together. Add 1 tbsp. melt butter and 1 teaspoon. vanilla.
8. To achieve a drizzling consistency, add milk as necessary.

Poop Emoji Cookies

Ingredients:

2 1/2 cups all-purpose flour
1 cup confectioners' sugar
3/4 cup unsweetened cocoa powder
2 tbsps. unsweetened cocoa powder
4 tsps. baking powder
2 tsps. vanilla sugar
1 pinch salt
9 tbsps. unsalted butter, cubed
1/4 cup milk
1 egg Decoration:
3 tbsps. confectioners' sugar
2 tsps. lemon juice, or as needed
90 candy eyeballs

Directions:

1. Combine flour, 1 cup confectioners' sugar, 3/4 cups plus 2 tbsps. In a large bowl, combine cocoa powder, baking flour, vanilla sugar, salt, and 2 tbsps.
2. Use your fingers to work butter into the mixture until it resembles fine crumbs.
3. Mix in milk and eggs and knead to a soft dough.
4. Cover the bowl with a lid and let it cool in the refrigerator for 30 minutes.
5. Preheat oven to 375°F (190° C).
6. Line 2 baking sheets using parchment paper.
7. Make long, narrow 8-inch ropes from the dough. Then pinch one end to make a pointed tip.
8. Place the cookies in the form of a little poop-mound, with the pointed tip at the top.
9. Bake for 10-12 minutes in the preheated oven, until the bottom is lightly darkened and the cake is dry.
10. Transfer the baking sheet to a wire rack and let cool on a wire rack for about 2 hours.
11. Combine 3 tablespoons. To make a thin frosting, mix confectioners' sugar and lemon juice.
12. Put 2 candy eyesballs on each poop cookie, and let dry.

Chocolate Halloween Cookies

Ingredients:

1 cup white sugar
2/3 cup butter, softened
1/3 cup milk
1 egg
1 1/2 tsps. vanilla extract
1 1/2 cups all-purpose flour
1/2 cup cocoa powder
1/2 tsp. baking powder
1/4 tsp. salt
1 cup candy-coated peanut butter pieces (such as Reese's Pieces®)

Frosting Ingredients:

3 tbsps. melted butter
3 tbsps. cocoa powder
1 cup confectioners' sugar
2 tbsps. milk
1/2 tsp. vanilla extract
1/4 cup candy-coated peanut butter pieces (such as Reese's Pieces)

Directions:

1. Preheat oven to 350°F (175° C).
2. Use an electric mixer to beat white sugar and 1/3 cup softened butter in a bowl until smooth and creamy
3. Add 1/3 cup milk, egg, 1 1/2 teaspoons, and vanilla extract. vanilla extract.
4. Mix flour, 1/2 cup cocoa powder and baking powder together in a creamed butter mixture. Fold in 1 cup candy-coated peanut Butter pieces.
5. Drop the dough, 1 to 2 tablespoons. per cookie, onto a baking sheet.
6. Bake the cookies in the oven for 10-12 minutes or until they are golden brown.
7. Let cookies cool in pans for about 2 to 3 minutes, then transfer to wire racks to cool completely.
8. Mix 3 tbsps. Melt butter and add 3 tbsps. Combine the cocoa powder and 3 tbsps butter in a bowl. Beat with an electric mixer until smooth. Add confectioners' sugar, 2 Tbsps. 1/2 tsp. milk. Vanilla extract until frosting becomes fluffy and smooth.
9. Frost cookies with peanut butter pieces coated in candy and decorate them with these peanut butter pieces.

Bloody Skeleton S'mores

Ingredients:

12 honey graham crackers
1 (1 oz.) tube black decorating gel
15 (1 oz.) squares dark chocolate
66 miniature marshmallows
6 skull-shaped candy decorations
1 tbsp. red cookie icing

Directions:

1. Use sharp kitchen scissors to cut 2 triangles from each corner of a rectangular Graham cracker.
2. To create a coffin shape, cut 2 long, thin triangles out of the bottom of the Graham cracker.
3. Continue with the remaining graham crackers, using the template from the first.
4. Place 6 graham crackers onto a plate.
5. Use the black decorating gel to draw crosses and "RIP" letters on each lid.
6. Split 3 squares of dark chocolate in half
7. Remaining 12 squares can be left unfinished.
8. Place the remaining 6 graham crackers onto a baking sheet.
9. Each square should contain 2 1/2 pieces of chocolate.
10. Place 11 mini marshmallows on top, in the form of a skeleton, 4 for the arms, 5 for your body and 2 for your legs.
11. Place oven rack 6 inches away from heat source. Preheat oven broiler to low setting.
12. Broil the graham cracker coffins until they turn a golden brown, about 10 to 20 seconds.
13. You can place skull candy above marshmallow skeletons.
14. Sprinkle red icing on top of the s'mores.
15. Sandwich the s'mores and the decorated graham cracker coffin covers.

S'mores Eyeballs

Ingredients:

8 whole graham crackers, crushed
6 tbsps. butter, melted
1/4 cup confectioners' sugar
2 (1.5 oz.) bars milk chocolate candy bars
12 large marshmallows, cut in half crosswise
1 dash red food coloring, or as needed
24 semisweet chocolate chips

Directions:

1. Preheat oven to 350°F (175° C).
2. Mix butter, graham cracker crumbs and confectioners' sugar in a bowl. Once the mixture is well combined, press it into a mini-muffin pan to make shallow cups.
3. Bake for 5 minutes in the preheated oven, or until edges are bubbling.
4. Each chocolate bar should be broken into 12 equal pieces. Place one of these pieces in each graham cracker cup.
5. Use red food coloring to paint red lines and circles on each marshmallow.
6. Place painted marshmallows upside down in graham cracker cups.
7. Place 1 chocolate chip in the middle of each marshmallow.
8. Bake marshmallows in the oven for 1 to 2 minutes or until they are lightly softened.
9. Allow to cool in the pan for 15 minutes, then remove.

Pumpkin Whoopie Pies

Ingredients:

2 cups packed brown sugar
1 cup vegetable oil
1 1/2 cups solid pack pumpkin puree
2 eggs
3 cups all-purpose flour
1 tsp. salt
1 tsp. baking powder
1 tsp. baking soda
1 tsp. vanilla extract
1 1/2 tbsps. ground cinnamon
1/2 tbsp. ground ginger
1/2 tbsp. ground cloves
1 egg white
2 tbsps. milk
1 tsp. vanilla extract
2 cups confectioners' sugar
3/4 cup shortening

Directions:

1. Preheat oven to 350°F (175° C).
2. Lightly grease baking sheets
3. Combine the oil, brown sugar and mustard. Beat in the eggs and pumpkin. Mix in the flour, salt and baking powder. Add 1 teaspoon baking soda. Add the vanilla, ginger, cinnamon, and cloves. Mix thoroughly.
4. Use a heap of tsps to drop the dough. Place the dough on the baking sheets.
5. Bake at 350°F (175°C) for 10-12 minutes.
6. Allow cookies to cool, then make sandwiches with two Whoopie Pie Filling cookies.
7. How to Make Whoopie Pie Filling
8. Mix egg white with milk. Vanilla and 1 cup confectioners' sugar.
9. Combine the ingredients and beat in the confectioners' sugar.
10. Mix until fluffy and light.

Booger Cookies

Ingredients:

1 cup margarine, softened
1/3 cup confectioners' sugar
1 egg
1 tsp. vanilla extract
3/4 tsp. almond extract
1 (3 oz.) pkg. instant pistachio pudding mix
2 cups all-purpose flour
1/2 cup semisweet chocolate chips
1 1/2 cups confectioners' sugar
1 tsp. vanilla extract
1 tbsp. milk, or as needed
3 drops green food coloring, or as needed
24 milk chocolate candy kisses, unwrapped

Directions:

1. Preheat oven to 350°F (175° C).
2. Lightly grease a baking pan.
3. Blend the margarine with 1/3 cup confectioners sugar in a large bowl.
4. Mix in 1 teaspoon of egg. Mix in the vanilla extract and almond extract until well combined
5. Blend the pudding mixture until smooth.
6. Mix in the flour and stir until well combined. Add the chocolate chips and fold in, making sure to combine everything evenly.
7. Make 1-inch balls from the cookie dough and place them on the baking sheet.
8. To indent each cookie, use your thumb.
9. Bake for 10 to 14 minutes in the preheated oven.
10. Let the cookies cool on the baking sheets for one minute, then transfer them to a wire rack to cool completely.
11. As the cookies cool, make the filling. Mix 1 1/2 cups confectioners sugar with 1 teaspoon of water in a bowl. Vanilla extract, milk, food coloring.
12. To make the mixture more smooth, add additional milk.
13. Sprinkle a bit of the green filling on each cooled cookie and top it with a candy-covered kiss.

Sugar Wafer Frankenstein Cookies

Ingredients:

Chocolate sugar wafer cream cookies
Green candy melts
Chocolate sprinkles
Candy eye balls

Directions:
1. Heat oven to 350°F (175°C).
2. Lightly grease your baking pan.
3. Combine 1/3 cup confectioners sugar and the margarine in a large bowl.
4. Add 1 teaspoon of egg. Combine the almond extract and vanilla extract until combined
5. Mix the pudding until smooth.
6. Add the flour to the bowl and stir until combined. Fold in the chocolate chips.
7. Roll 1-inch balls of cookie dough and place them onto a baking sheet.
8. Use your thumb to indent each cookie.
9. Bake in the oven for 10-14 minutes.
10. Allow the cookies to cool on baking sheets for 1 minute. Then transfer them to a wire rack and let cool completely.
11. Make the filling once the cookies have cooled. Combine 1 1/2 cups confectioners sugar and 1 teaspoon water in a bowl. Add vanilla extract, milk, and food coloring.
12. Add milk to make the mixture smoother.
13. Spread a little of the green filling onto each cooled cookie, and then top it off with a candy-covered Kiss.

Vampire Bite Sugar Cookies

Ingredients:

3 1/4 cup flour
1 tsp baking soda
1/2 tsp. salt
1 tsp. nutmeg
1 tsp. baking powder
1/2 cup Butter
1 cup sugar
1 egg
1 tsp. vanilla
1/2 cup thick sour cream
Seedless raspberry jelly
vanilla sugar

Directions:

1. Preheat the oven to 350°F
2. Mix the flour, baking soda and salt together.
3. In a separate bowl, beat the Butter, sugar and egg.
4. Combine the dry ingredients with the wet ingredients until well combined.
5. Divide into four flat disks and wrap with wax paper. Refrigerate for 4 hours or overnight.
6. The dough should be rolled out between sheets of parchment paper. It should be thinner than normal and less than 1/4 inch.
7. Make your circles, and then spread them out a bit. Roll them out until they measure about 1/8 inch.
8. Place a little jelly in half of the circles. Next, top each jelly circle by placing one of the plain circles on top.
9. To seal the layers, cut the cookies once more.
10. Sprinkle the vanilla sugar over the top for a sweet crunch.
11. To create teeth marks, use a toothpick to break through the jelly's top layer twice.
12. Bake for 12-15 minutes, or until edges are lightly golden.
13. Allow to cool, then add some jelly "dripping" from your teeth marks.

Chocolate Chip Spider Cookies

Ingredients:

2 cups + 2 tbsp all-purpose flour
½ tsp baking soda
½ tsp salt
12 tbsps. butter
1 melted and cooled until warm
1 cup brown sugar
½ cup granulated sugar
1 large egg + 1 egg yolk
2 tsp vanilla extract
2 cups semi-sweet chocolate chips divided

Directions:

1. To heat oven, heat to 325°F
2. Mix flour, salt, baking soda, and milk in a large bowl.
3. Use an electric mixer to combine the butter and sugars in a large bowl.
4. Mix the egg, egg yolk, vanilla and milk together. Mix in the dry ingredients until well combined.
5. Mix 3/4 cup of chocolate chips into the dough. Once the dough is incorporated, it will become soft.
6. Make small balls of the dough and place them on a parchment-lined cookie sheet.
7. Bake for between 10-12 minutes. Take out of the oven and add 3-4 chocolate chips to each cookie's tops, pointed side up.
8. Place remaining chocolate chips in a microwave-safe bowl. Microwave on low power for 30 seconds, stirring after each 30 second, until the chocolate is melted.
9. You should just trim the corner of a small ziplock bag. This will allow you to make spider legs.
10. Use the bag to place the melted chocolate in and draw spider legs along the sides of the chocolate chips.
11. Cookies can be stored in an airtight container, or frozen in a freezer ziplock bag.

Double Chocolate Halloween Cookies

Ingredients:

2 cups flour
2/3 cup unsweetened cocoa powder
1 tsp. baking soda
1/4 tsp. salt
1 cup (2 sticks) butter, softened
1 cup granulated sugar
2/3 cup firmly packed light brown sugar
2 eggs
2 tsps. vanilla extract
1 cup chocolate chips
1 cup Halloween colored Sixlets

Directions:

1. Preheat oven to 350°F
2. In a medium bowl, combine flour, baking soda, and cocoa powder. Set aside.
3. Use an electric mixer to beat butter and sugars until they are light and fluffy.
4. Mix in vanilla and eggs. Slowly add flour mixture, beating on low speed until it is well combined.
5. Add Sixlets and chocolate chips to the mixture.
6. Drop by rounded tablespoons. Place about 2 inches apart on baking sheets. Spray with no stick cooking spray.
7. Bake for 8-10 minutes, or until the cookies are golden brown.
8. Allow to cool on baking sheets for 2 minutes.
9. Transfer to wire racks and let cool completely.

Dracula's Dentures

Ingredients:

1 pkg. (16.5 oz.) refrigerated chocolate chip cookie bar dough
1/2 cup prepared vanilla frosting, tinted red or pink
1 3/4 cups miniature marshmallows
48 blanched slivered almonds

Directions:

1. Bake cookies according to the instructions on the package.
2. Allow to cool on baking sheets for two minutes.
3. Transfer to a wire rack to cool completely. Each cookie should be cut in half, for 48 total halves.
4. Frost the bottoms of all cookie halves using frosting
5. Place six marshmallow teeth around the curved perimeter of 24 halves.
6. Add the remaining 24 halves.
7. An additional marshmallow can be added behind the teeth to provide additional support.
8. For fangs, insert two almond slivers between your teeth.
9. Dip tips in frosting if fangs don't stick.

Halloween Pinwheel Cookies

Ingredients:

5 cups flour
2 tsp. baking powder
1 tsp. salt
1 1/2 cup butter, softened
2 cups granulated sugar
4 eggs
1 tsp. vanilla
Purple gel food coloring
Green gel food coloring

Directions:

1. Use a hand mixer to combine the softened butter and sugar in a bowl until it is smooth.
2. Mix in eggs.
3. Mix the vanilla with the water.
4. Mix together flour, baking powder, salt in a separate bowl.
5. Continue to mix the dry mixture with the wet until everything is well combined.
6. Divide the dough in half, and then place them in separate bowls.
7. Mix the green gel food coloring in one bowl. Use your hands to evenly distribute the color throughout the dough.
8. Continue with the purple in the second bowl.
9. Each batch of dough should be rolled into a ball, then wrapped in plastic wrap.
10. Keep it in the refrigerator for at least one hour
11. Dust the counter, cutting board, and rolling pin with flour.
12. Cover the purple dough ball with flour.
13. Roll the rolling pin, and then leave it on the counter.
14. Cover the ball of green dough with flour and unwrap it.
15. It can be rolled out on a new cutting board or counter.
16. You can lift the green dough from the counter with a spatula and place it on top of purple dough.
17. Roll the dough using the rolling pin.
18. To create a rectangle shape, remove any excess dough.
19. The dough should be rolled into a log. Wrap it in plastic wrap. Make sure you wrap the log in plastic wrap.
20. Put the dough in the freezer for one hour.
21. Turn oven on to 325 degrees
22. Take out the frozen dough and take off the plastic wrap
23. Cut into 2-inch slices while keeping the circle shape.
24. Place slices on a parchment-lined cookie sheet.
25. Bake for 13-15 minutes
26. Let it cool down and then enjoy!

White Chocolate Reese's Pieces Peanut Butter Chip Cookies

Ingredients:

2 1/2 cups all-purpose flour
1 tsp. baking soda
1/2 tsp. salt
2 sticks (8 oz.) unsalted butter, at room temperature
1 cup + 2 tbsps. light brown sugar, packed
1/2 cup granulated sugar
2 tsps. vanilla
2 large eggs, at room temperature
1 cup white chocolate chips
1 cup peanut butter chips
1/2 cup Reese's Pieces

Directions:

1. Preheat oven to 375°F
2. Place 2 large baking sheets on parchment paper.
3. Mix the flour, baking soda and sea salt in a medium bowl.
4. Mix the butter, sugar, vanilla and butter in a large bowl. Whisk until light and fluffy, approximately 2 minutes.
5. Mix the eggs together and continue beating for about 30 seconds, until they are just combined.
6. Allow the mixture to rest for five minutes. Then beat the eggs for 30 seconds more.
7. Use a rubber spatula to gently fold the flour mixture in, stirring only until it disappears completely.
8. Add white chocolate, peanut butter chips and Reese's Pieces.
9. 3. Tbsp. Make 3 tablespoons of dough. Roll them between your palms until they form a ball.
10. Continue to do this until you have all of the dough rolled.
11. Bake for 11 minutes on baking sheets.
12. Allow cookies to cool on a baking sheet for five minutes before moving to a wire rack.

Skeleton Oreo Pops

Ingredients:

12 Halloween Oreos
2 c. white chocolate, melted
2 tsp. coconut oil
Black icing
12 lollipop sticks
Black ribbon

Directions:

1. Place parchment paper on a baking sheet medium.
2. Stick the lollipop sticks in the cream of the Oreos.
3. Coconut oil and white chocolate can be combined. Dip Oreos in chocolate until coated completely. Allow to set in the refrigerator for 5-10 minutes.
4. Use the black icing to draw Jack's face onto the Oreos. Let cool.
5. Serve by tying a black ribbon with a bow at bottom of Oreo.

Mini Mummy Cookie Pops

Ingredients:

1 pouch sugar cookie mix
Butter and egg called for on cookie mix pouch
1 cup creamy peanut butter
1 package (20 oz.) vanilla-flavored candy coating (almond bark)
72 candy eyeballs
48 paper lollipop sticks

Directions:

1. Heat oven to 350 degrees F.
2. Make cookie dough as directed on cookie mix pouch.
3. Roll level tsps. of dough between hands to form balls.
4. Place balls 1 inch apart on ungreased cookie sheets.
5. Press paper lollipop stick into half the cookies.
6. Bake 8 to 10 minutes or until edges are golden brown.
7. Cool on cookie sheets 5 minutes; cool completely on cooling rack, about 30 minutes.
8. Spread 1 tsp. peanut butter on cookies with lollipop sticks; top with remaining cookies to make sandwiches.
9. Melt almond bark as directed on package in 2-cup glass measuring cup or microwavable bowl.
10. Carefully dip each cookie sandwich into melted almond bark to coat completely.
11. Cool completely on waxed paper, about 20 minutes.
12. Place remaining melted almond bark in re-sealable plastic food storage bag. Cut off one small corner.
13. Drizzle melted almond bark over cookie sandwiches to look like mummy bandages.
14. Press 2 candy eyeballs into each of the cookies.
15. Cool completely, about 1 hour.

Halloween Macaroons

Ingredients:

2 large egg whites
1/2 cup sugar
1 tsp. vanilla extract
1/4 tsp. cream of tartar
1/8 tsp. salt
2-3/4 cups sweetened shredded coconut
1/3 cup candy corn, chopped
1/4 cup dark chocolate chips
1/4 cup peanut butter chips
1/4 cup finely chopped macadamia nuts
2/3 cup white baking chips, melted

Directions:

Preheat oven to 300°F

Mix the first five ingredients in a small bowl until well combined. Mix the coconut, peanut butter chips, dark chocolate chips, and candy corn in a large bowl. Add the egg white mixture.

Drop 12 cupfuls. Place on parchment-lined baking sheets. Bake for 20-22 minutes, or until light brown.

To cool completely, transfer pans to wire racks.

Let the cookies cool before you drizzle them with melted baking chips.

Ghost Shortbread Cookies

Ingredients:

1 cup butter, softened
1 cup confectioners' sugar
2 cups all-purpose flour
1/2 cup cornstarch
Orange and blue food coloring, optional

Frosting Ingredients:

- 1-1/3 cups confectioners' sugar 1/4 cup butter, softened
- 2-1/2 tsps. milk

Directions for 60 mini semisweet chocolate chips

1. Preheat oven to 325° F
2. Beat butter, cornstarch, and confectioners' sugar together in a large bowl until well blended. Gradually add flour. Divide the dough in half and tint one side with orange or blue if desired. Roll each piece of dough 1/4 inch on a floured surface. Thickness
3. Use a floured 2-in. tulip-shaped cookie cutter.
4. Place 2 in. Place 2 in.
5. Bake for 7-9 minutes, or until the bottoms are lightly brown.
6. To cool completely, transfer pans to wire racks.
7. Combine butter, confectioners' sugar and milk in a small bowl; mix until smooth.
8. Add eyes to each ghost and top with chocolate chips. Allow to set.

Halloween Black Cat Cookies

Ingredients:

1 cup chunky peanut butter
2 eggs
1/3 cup water
1 package chocolate cake mix
Sugar
90 M&M's minis (about 2 tbsps.)
60 pieces (3/4 inch) black licorice
Directions:

1. Preheat oven to 375°F
2. Mix peanut butter, eggs, and water in a large bowl until well combined. Gradually add the cake mix.
3. Shape into 1-1/2-in. Place 2 in. balls on a plate. Place 2 in. apart on greased baking pans. Use a glass of sugar to flatten the cookies. To make ears, pinch the top of the cookie.
4. Bake for 10-12 minutes, or until the bottoms are slightly browned and set. Take out of oven and immediately apply M&M's to eyes and noses.
5. For whiskers, add licorice.
6. Allow to cool on wire racks.

Day of the Dead Cookies

Ingredients:

1-1/4 cups butter, softened
1-3/4 cups confectioners' sugar
2 oz. almond paste
1 large egg
1/4 cup 2% milk
1 tsp. vanilla extract
4 cups all-purpose flour
1/2 tsp. salt
2 packages (12 oz. each) white candy coating melts
Decorations of your choice: jumbo sprinkles, peppermint candies, candy-coated sunflower kernels, Skittles, Twizzlers Rainbow Twists and Good & Plenty candies
Black paste food coloring
Directions:

1. In a large bowl, cream butter and confectioners' sugar until light and fluffy; add almond paste. Beat in the egg, milk and vanilla.
2. Combine flour and salt; gradually add to creamed mixture and mix well.
3. Cover and refrigerate for 1 hour.
4. On a lightly floured surface, roll out dough to 1/4-in. thickness.
5. Cut out with a floured 5-in. skull-shaped cookie cutter. Place 1 in. apart on ungreased baking sheets.
6. Bake at 375 degrees for 7-9 minutes or until firm.
7. Let stand for 2 minutes before removing to wire racks to cool completely.
8. In a large, shallow microwave-safe dish, melt white candy melts according to package directions.
9. Dip top side of each cookie into coating, allowing excess to drip off; place on waxed paper.
10. Add decorations as desired. Tint remaining white coating black; pipe on mouth.
11. Let stand until set.

Pumpkin Cookie Pops

Ingredients:

1/2 cup butter, softened
3/4 cup packed brown sugar
1/2 cup sugar
1 egg
1 tsp. vanilla extract
1 cup canned pumpkin
2-1/2 cups all-purpose flour
1 tsp. baking powder
1 tsp. baking soda
1 tsp. ground cinnamon
30 Popsicle sticks
1/3 cup green gumdrops, quartered lengthwise

Icing Ingredients:

4 cups confectioners' sugar
1/4 cup water
Orange, black, purple, green and red paste or gel food coloring

Directions:

1. In a large bowl, cream butter and sugars until light and fluffy. Beat in egg and vanilla. Beat in pumpkin. Combine the flour, baking powder, baking soda and cinnamon; gradually add to creamed mixture and mix well (dough will be soft).
2. Drop by rounded tablespoonfuls 2 in. apart onto greased or parchment paper-lined baking sheets.
3. Insert popsicle sticks into dough.
4. Insert a gumdrop piece into the top of each for the pumpkin stem.
5. Bake at 350° for 14-16 minutes or until set and lightly browned around the edges. Remove to wire racks to cool.
6. For icing, in a large bowl, combine confectioners' sugar and water until smooth.
7. Remove 1/2 cup to another bowl; cover and set aside.
8. Stir orange food coloring into remaining icing.
9. Spread or pipe over cookies. Let stand for 30 minutes or until icing is set and dry.
10. Tint reserved icing with colors of your choice; use colored icing to create jack-o'-lantern faces.

Bloody Bones Cookies

Ingredients:

5 large egg whites
1/2 cup cake flour
1/2 cup ground almonds
1/4 tsp. ground cinnamon
1/8 tsp. ground cloves
1/8 tsp. ground nutmeg
1 tsp. vanilla extract
1/4 tsp. cream of tartar
1 dash salt
4 drops yellow food coloring, optional
3/4 cup plus 2 tbsps. sugar

Sauce Ingredients:

1-1/4 cups heavy whipping cream
1/2 cup semisweet chocolate chips
1/2 cup strawberry jelly
Red food coloring, optional

Directions:

1. Place egg whites in a large bowl; let stand at room temperature for 30 minutes. Meanwhile, combine the flour, almonds, cinnamon, cloves and nutmeg.
2. Add the vanilla, cream of tartar, salt and, if desired, food coloring to the egg whites.
3. Beat on medium speed until soft peaks form.
4. Gradually add sugar, 1 tbsp. at a time, beating on high until stiff glossy peaks form and sugar is dissolved.
5. Fold in flour mixture.
6. Cut a 1/2-in. hole in the corner of a pastry or plastic bag.
7. Fill bag with egg white mixture.
8. Pipe 4-in. logs onto parchment-lined baking sheets.
9. Pipe two 1/2-in. balls at both ends of each log.
10. Bake at 300 degrees F for 25-30 minutes or until firm to the touch.
11. Remove to wire racks.
12. In a small microwave-safe bowl, combine the cream, chocolate chips and jelly.
13. Microwave on high in 30-second intervals until melted.
14. Stir until smooth.
15. Tint red if desired.
16. Cool to room temperature and serve with bones.
17. Refrigerate leftover sauce.

Gingerbread Skeletons

Ingredients:

2/3 cup shortening
1/2 cup sugar
1/2 cup molasses
1 large egg
3 cups all-purpose flour
1 tsp. baking soda
1 tsp. each ground cinnamon, ginger and cloves
1/2 tsp. salt
1/2 tsp. ground nutmeg
Confectioners' sugar icing

Directions:

1. In a bowl, cream shortening and sugar.
2. Add molasses and egg; mix well.
3. Combine flour, baking soda, cinnamon, ginger, cloves, salt and nutmeg; gradually add to creamed mixture and mix well.
4. Divide dough in half. Refrigerate at least 2 hours.
5. Preheat oven to 350°. On a lightly floured surface, roll out each portion of dough to 1/8-in. thickness.
6. Cut with a floured 2-in. cookie cutter. Place 2 in. apart on greased baking sheets.
7. Bake 9 minutes or until edges are firm.
8. Remove to wire racks to cool. Decorate as desired.

Chocolate Peanut Butter Owl Cookies

Ingredients:

2/3 cup butter, softened
1 cup creamy peanut butter
1 cup packed brown sugar
1 large egg
1 tsp. vanilla extract
1-1/3 cups all-purpose flour
1 cup quick-cooking oats
1 tsp. baking powder
1/2 tsp. salt
1 oz. unsweetened chocolate, melted
12 whole cashews
24 striped chocolate kisses, unwrapped
24 semisweet chocolate chips

Directions:

1. In a large bowl, beat butter, peanut butter and brown sugar until blended.
2. Beat in egg and vanilla. In another bowl, mix flour, oats, baking powder and salt; gradually beat into creamed mixture.
3. If necessary, cover and refrigerate dough 1 hour or until firm enough to shape.
4. Divide dough in half; shape one portion into an 8-in. long roll.
5. Mix melted chocolate into remaining dough.
6. Roll chocolate dough between two sheets of waxed paper into an 8-in. square. Place plain roll on chocolate dough. Wrap chocolate dough around plain dough, pinching together at the seam to seal.
7. Wrap in plastic; refrigerate 3 hours or until firm.
8. Preheat oven to 350°. Unwrap and cut dough crosswise into 24 slices 3/8 in. thick.
9. To make owls, place two slices side by side on an ungreased baking sheet; pinch the top of each slice for ears. Place a cashew between slices for a beak.
10. Repeat with remaining dough.
11. Bake 12-15 minutes or until set.
12. Cool on pans 5 minutes before removing to wire racks.
13. While cookies are warm, place two kisses on each cookie, pointed side down, for eyes. (Kisses will melt slightly.)
14. Top each kiss with a chocolate chip. Cool completely. Yield: 1 dozen.

Oreo Pumpkin Cookie Balls

Ingredients:

6 oz. cream cheese, softened
1 pkg. (15.25 oz.) Oreo Peanut Butter Creme Cookies, finely crushed
3 pkg. (4 oz. each) Baker's White Chocolate, broken into pieces, melted
1 cup orange colored sugar
10 pretzel sticks, each broken into 4 pieces

Directions:

1. Mix cream cheese and cookie crumbs until blended.
2. Shape into 40 (1-inch) balls.
3. Dip balls in melted chocolate; roll in sugar to evenly coat.
4. Place in single layer in shallow waxed paper-lined pan.
5. Insert 1 pretzel piece into top of each for the pumpkin's stem.
6. Refrigerate 1 hour or until firm.

Chocolate Bat Cookies

Ingredients:

2/3 cup shortening
1 cup sugar
1 egg
1 cup (6 oz.) semisweet chocolate chips, melted
1 tsp. vanilla extract
1/2 tsp. almond extract
1 cup all-purpose flour
1 cup quick-cooking oats
1 tsp. salt
1/2 tsp. baking soda
1 cup sweetened shredded coconut, finely chopped
Red-hot candies

9 798497 520972